Dreamtivity

# Shadow Match

## Which is the sea lion's exact shadow?

DreamTivity

# Make It Rhyme

**Can you think of 5 words that rhyme with:**

# TREE

_____

_____

_____

_____

_____

# BIGGEST
## Christmas List EVER!

Dear Santa,

i've been good!
Here is my list.

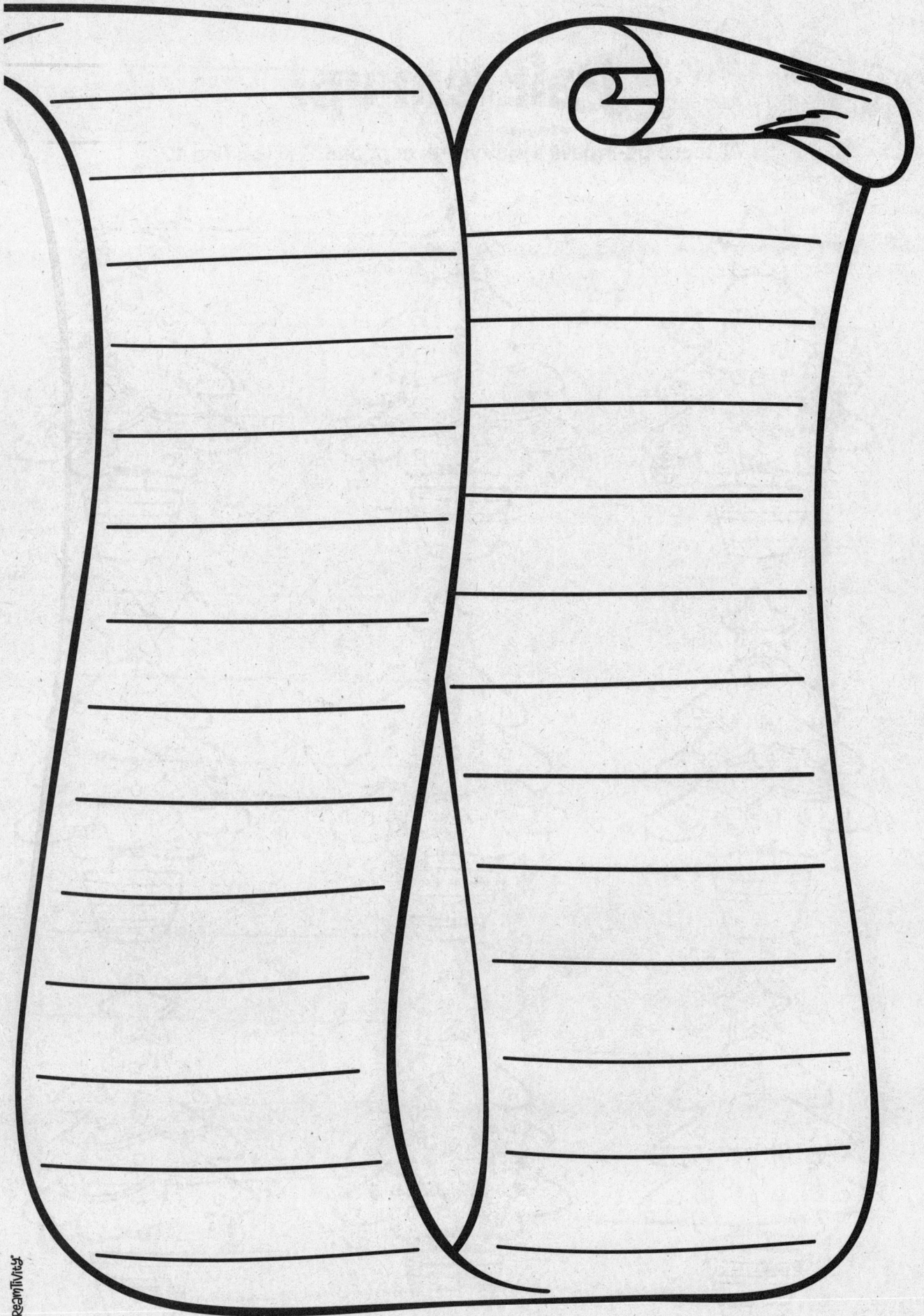

# Pair 'em up!

**All these trees have a match—except one. Can you find it?**

# Ribbon Squiggles!

## What do you see in the shape of the ribbon? Draw it!

Dreamtivity

# So warm...so festive!

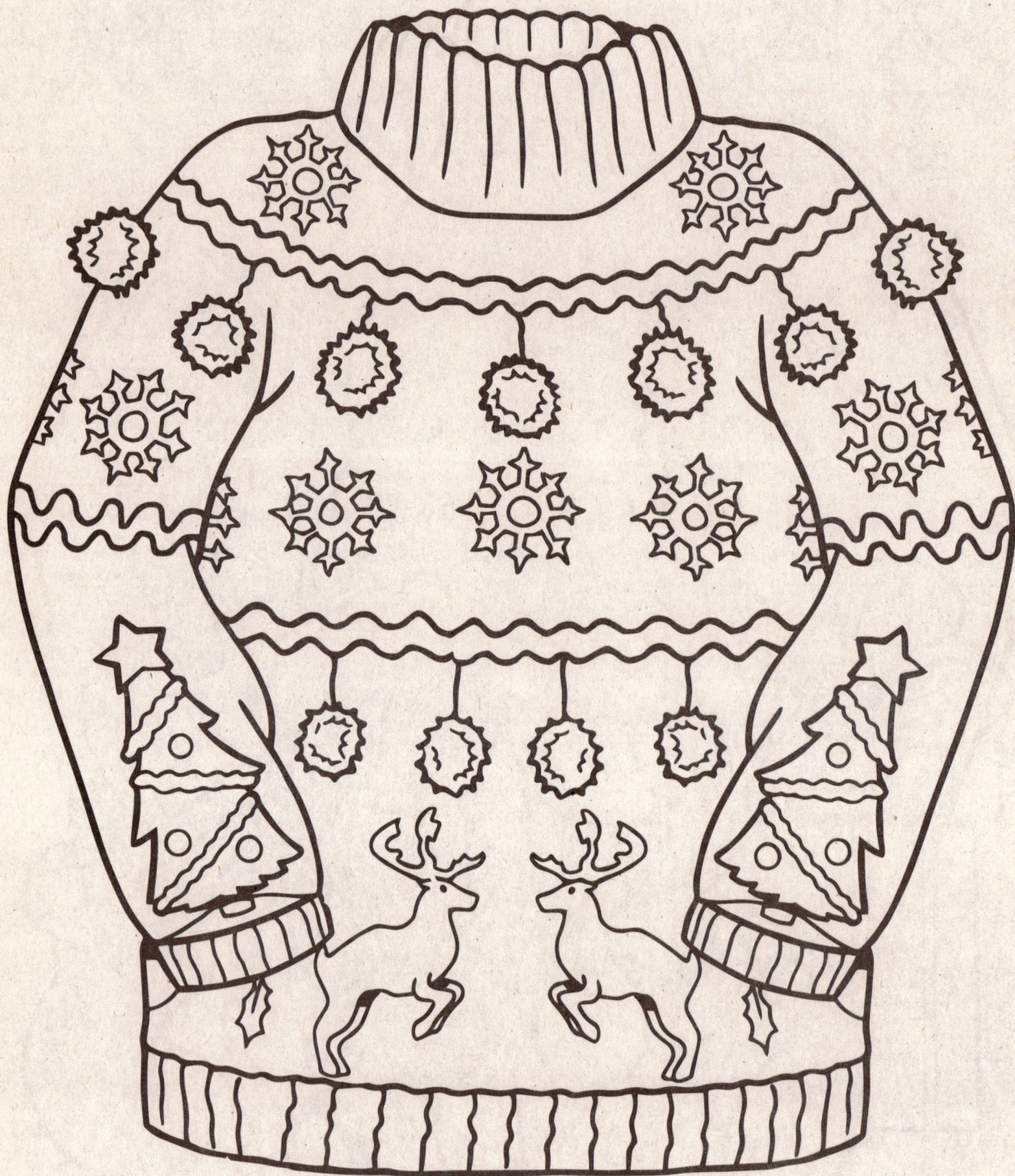

# Design a sweater!

Use festive patterns to design your own.

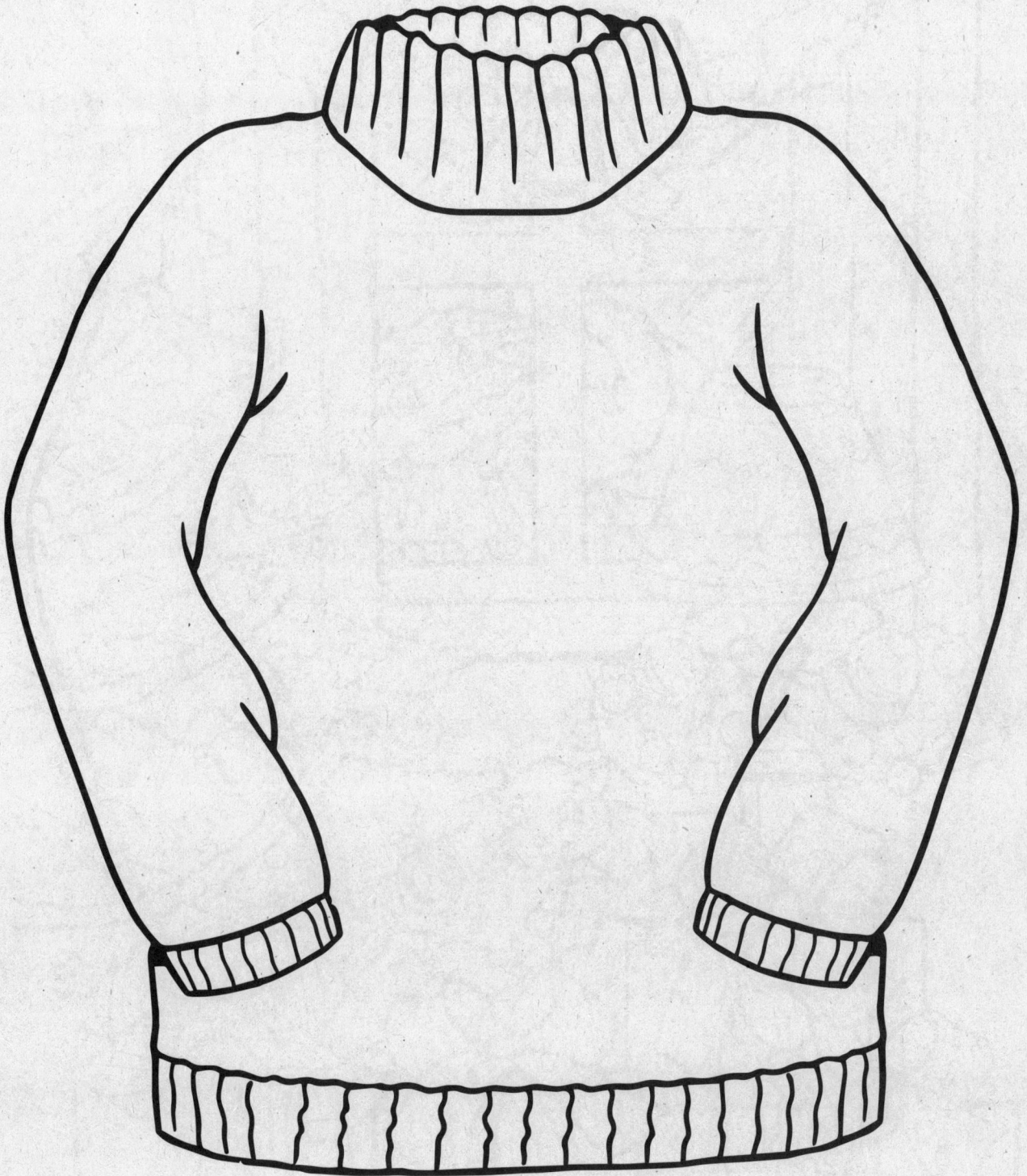

# Christmas Eve Word Search

Look up, down, across, diagonally, and backward. Can you find these words in the puzzle?

CANDLES   FAMILY   PEACE
SING   SLEEPY
SNUGGLE   SPECIAL   STORY

```
F A M I L Y E   E
L E R C P S   L
O P Y E E I   G
O V O E R S N G
E L S A O G U
S O N M C T N
C A N D L E S
L A I C E P S
```

# Gnome Sweet Gnome

### Design a gnome hat!

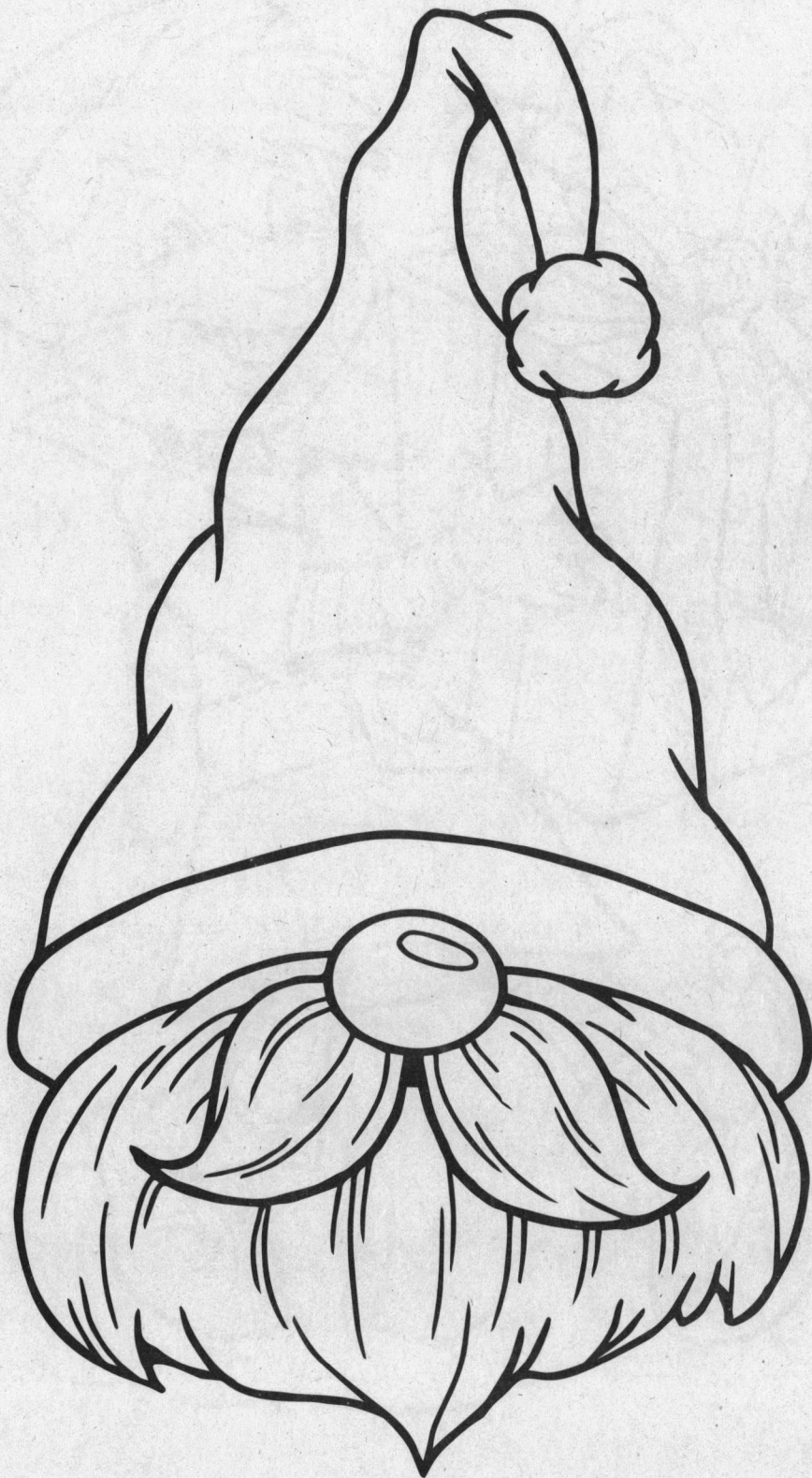

# Gnomes Galore! Word Search

**Look up, down, across, diagonally, and backward. How many times can you find the word:**

## GNOME

| | | | | | | | |
|---|---|---|---|---|---|---|---|
| E | M | O | N | G | R | S |
| G | R | D | J | G | A | G |
| T | N | B | L | N | N | E |
| U | G | O | B | O | Q | M |
| C | N | H | M | M | S | O |
| L | O | E | Q | E | F | N |
| V | M | Y | I | P | V | G |
| F | E | M | O | N | G | K |

# Complete it!

**Which 3 pieces complete the picture?**

A

B

C

D

E

**Your answers:**

# Follow the Path

**Which line leads to the lollipop?**

① ② ③ ④

Answer: 2

# Dear Santa,

my name is _____

i am _____ years old.

This year i have been:

☐ goooooood — all of the time ☐ good — sometimes

☐ good — most of the time ☐ naughty (but nice)

This Christmas, it would be super if you could bring me these things:

_____

_____

_____

_____

thank you! you are the best Santa ever!

With love, _____

P.S. please tell mrs. claus and the elves _____

_____ for me. Thanks!

DreamTivity

# So many words!

How many words can you make using the letters in:

# HAPPY HOLIDAYS

_____

_____

_____

_____

_____

_____

_____

_____

# Spot the differences

**Find 5 things different between these scenes.**

# Maze

**Help the gnome find the gifts.**

START

FINISH

# Let it Snow! Word Search

Look up, down, across, diagonally, and backward. Can you find these words in the puzzle?

BOOTS   MITTENS   SCARF
WINTER   SLED   SNOWBALL
SNOWMAN   WOOL CAP

```
S  N  E  T  T  I  M
N  A  M  W  O  N  S
O  R  D  O  E  E  F
W  E  S  O  Z  R  S
B  T  L  L  A  T  T
A  N  S  C  E  I  O
L  I  S  A  M  D  O
L  W  B  P  Z  T  B
```

# Ribbon Squiggles!

**What do you see in the shape of the ribbon? Draw it!**

# Find the Match

**Which two sloths are an exact match?**

A

B

C

D

Your Answer

[ ] & [ ]

# A Christmas Village

Display a Christmas Village in your room.
Color the 8 village buildings on the next pages.
Carefully remove the pages and line them up on your wall.
How festive!

OLD TIME CANDY SHOP

# Shadow Match

### Which is the girl's exact shadow?

A

B

C

# A MERRY FAIRY

Draw a face and draw a pattern on the fairy's dress and wings.

# Pair 'em up!

All these gnomes have a match—except one. Can you find him?

BOOKSHOP

SALE
TODAY

# So many words!

How many words can you make using the letters in:

## GNOME FOR THE HOLIDAYS

_____

_____

_____

_____

_____

_____

_____

SOUVENIR SHOP

OPEN

Dreamtivity

# Maze

Help the hippo find another present.

Start

Finish

THE Village
FLOWERS & GIFTS

# How Many Stars

How many stars do you count?

# Complete it!

## Which 3 pieces complete the picture?

**A**

**B**

**C**

**D**

**E**

**Your answers:**

Dreamtivity

# Ready for Santa

# Design a stocking!

Use festive patterns to design your own.

# Color-By-Number

Use the code to color the picture.

| 1 | 2 | 3 | 4 | 5 | 6 | 7 | 8 |
|---|---|---|---|---|---|---|---|
| red | orange | yellow | light blue | blue | light green | green | purple |

# Find the Match

### Which two snow fairies are an exact match?

**A**

**B**

**C**

**D**

**Your Answer**

◻ & ◻

Answer: A & B

# Ha-Ha-Ha-Ho-Ho!

## What is a gnome's favorite Christmas movie?

Use the code to find the answer.

| G | L | E | A | M | O | N |
|---|---|---|---|---|---|---|

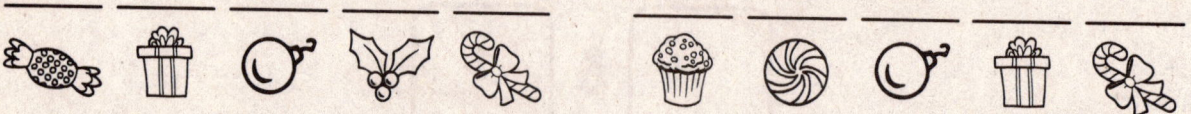

# Find the Match

## Which two gnomes are an exact match?

A

B

C

D

**Your Answer**

☐ & ☐

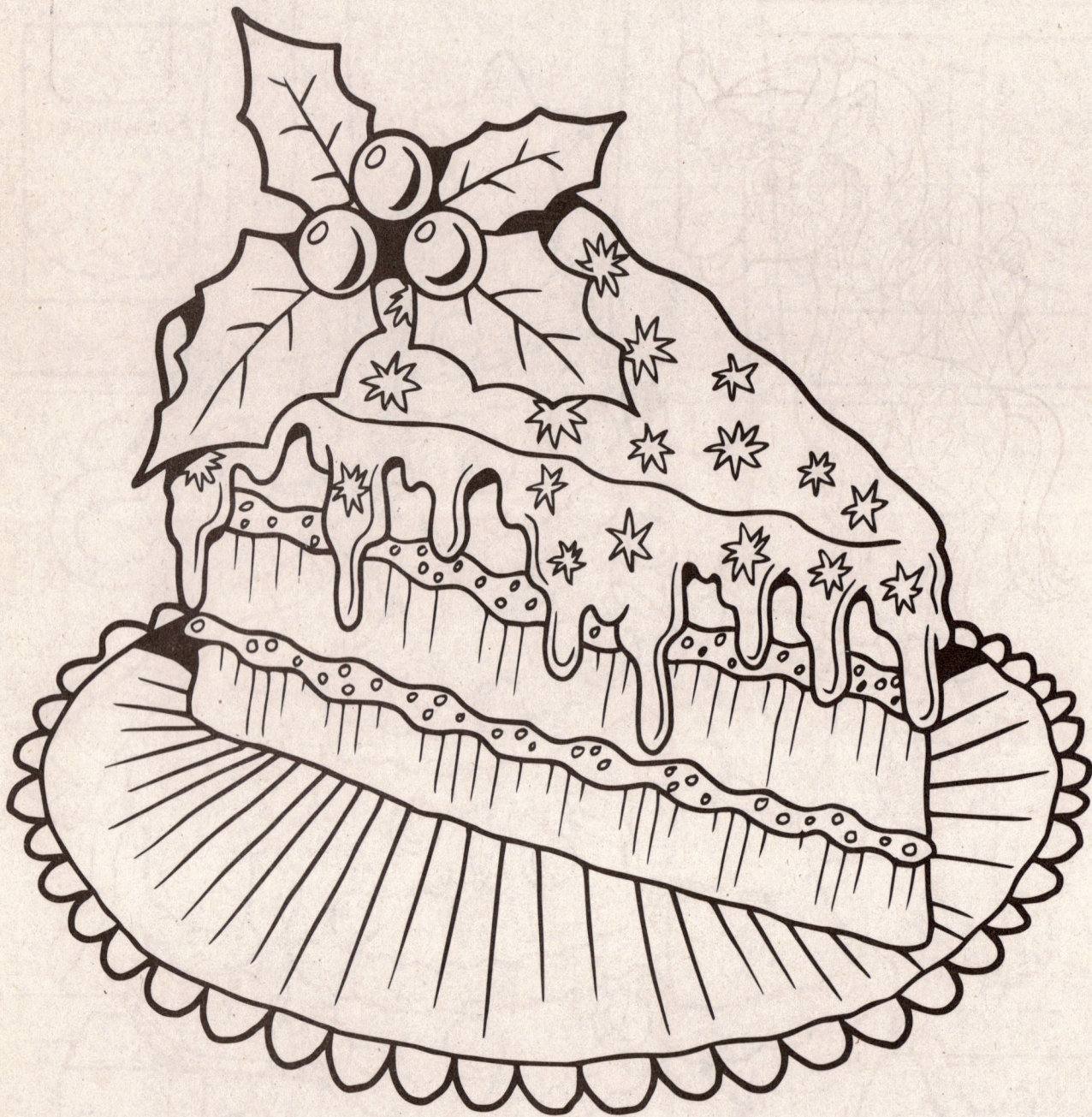

# Follow the Path

### Which line leads the giraffe to the Christmas tree?

**Your Answer**

**1.**

**2.**

**3.**

# Shadow Match

**Which is the squirrel's exact shadow?**

A

B

C

Answer: A

MERRY CHRISTMAS

# Complete it!

**Which 3 pieces complete the picture?**

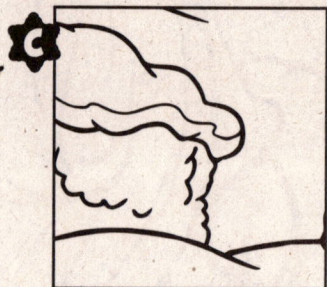

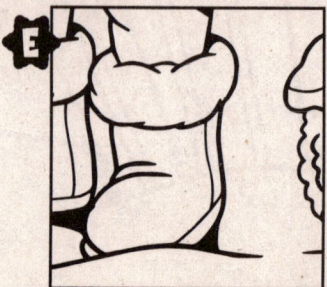

A

B

C

D

E

**Your answers:**

# Exact Match

**Draw a line from each nutcracker to its exact match!**

# Time to Rhyme

**Can you think of 5 words that rhyme with:**

# BRIGHT

_____

_____

_____

_____

_____

DreamTivity

# HEY, KIDS! WE WANT TO SEE YOUR CREATIVITY!

# Be part of TeamTivity™*

We love seeing your work! Color or complete a favorite page from any Dreamtivity book. Have a grown-up photograph or scan it, and share your masterpiece with the team. It's that easy! You never know, we might display it for all to see!

## NOW, GO COLOR YOUR WORLD!

Upload your art to: facebook.com/dreamtivity
Or email it to: teamtivity@dreamtivity.net
*Be sure to include your child's first name and age.
Tell us your favorite thing to color.*

*TeamTivity is our fun connection with creative kids everywhere!
We aim to inspire, encourage and champion their creativity!

**DreamTivity®**

**TeamTivity™**
**CREATIVE KID!**

YOUR NAME _____
I sent my masterpiece on _____
and now I am a part of the team!                DATE

**DreamTivity®**  NOW, GO COLOR YOUR WORLD!

Cut along dashed line and keep for yourself.